Original title:
The Connectivity Conundrum

Copyright © 2024 Swan Charm
All rights reserved.

Author: Johan Kirsipuu
ISBN HARDBACK: 978-9916-86-569-9
ISBN PAPERBACK: 978-9916-86-570-5
ISBN EBOOK: 978-9916-86-571-2

Symphonies of the Solipsistic

In the silence, thoughts collide,
A symphony of one abides.
Melodies that echo, true,
Existence felt in shades of blue.

Notes of longing drift away,
Softly whispering what they say.
In this realm of self-defined,
The world outside feels far behind.

Fingers dance on empty air,
Crafting dreams with utmost care.
Each heartbeat a familiar song,
In my mind, I can't go wrong.

Yet in shadows, whispers creep,
Secrets buried, buried deep.
The symphony starts to fade,
As the night begins to invade.

Still, the music calls me near,
In solitude, I find my cheer.
A blend of hope, of fear, of light,
In solipsism's endless night.

Tangles of Togetherness

Hands entwined, a gentle squeeze,
In moments caught, hearts find ease.
Laughter blooms like flowers bright,
In the warmth of shared delight.

Paths that twist, a dance of fate,
Together, we navigate.
Every glance a silent vow,
In this present, here and now.

Whispers soft as silken threads,
Bind our stories, where love spreads.
In the chaos, we find peace,
From the world, we seek release.

Yet storms may cloud our sunny days,
Through the struggles, love still stays.
Tangled roots, we grow as one,
In togetherness, we've begun.

Through every challenge, side by side,
In our hearts, we shall confide.
Tangled paths that intertwine,
Together, we will always shine.

Virtual Embraces

Across the screens, we bridge the gap,
In pixels wrapped, within the map.
Voices travel through the air,
In the virtual, we lay bare.

Fingers glide on glassy floors,
In this realm, imagination soars.
Every smile, a spark ignites,
Creating warmth on lonely nights.

Yet with the light, shadows blend,
Virtual touches that can't transcend.
Truths can hide behind the screen,
In this world, what's truly seen?

Embraces wrapped in codes and file,
Distance dulled by our shared smile.
A tapestry of hearts and dreams,
In the web, nothing's as it seems.

Still, we yearn for something real,
For the warmth that we can feel.
In the virtual, we take our place,
Hoping for that real embrace.

Ghosts in the Machine

Whispers echo, circuits hum,
In the silence, they become.
Shadows flicker, souls awake,
Ghosts among the tools we make.

In wires, secrets softly flow,
Digital tunes that never show.
A haunting trace of life once lived,
In every byte, a memory give.

Searching for a touch of grace,
Finding warmth in empty space.
Binary heartbeats, pulse in time,
The others hide in coded rhyme.

Yet in this realm, we feel alive,
With every thought, we learn, survive.
Connections forged in endless streams,
Amidst the data, we find dreams.

Through the mist, we reach for light,
As the ghosts whisper through the night.
In the machine, we find our way,
Dancing shadows, come what may.

Wires in the Clouds

Wires weave through the sky,
Connecting dreams up high.
Whispers lost in the breeze,
Floating with such ease.

Caught in a tangled mess,
No more time to stress.
The city sparkles bright,
In the soft moonlight.

Fingers dance through air,
Wishing without a care.
Hopes like clouds above,
Carried on beams of love.

Towers stand tall and proud,
Veils of silver shroud.
Voices intermingle fast,
Present, future, past.

Electric dreams ignite,
Guiding through the night.
Wires whisper unseen,
In this vast machine.

Threads of Invisible Ties

Threads connect us all,
In the silent hall.
Invisible yet real,
Emotions we conceal.

Fingers stretch so wide,
In hearts, we confide.
Moments rise like smoke,
Binding words unspoke.

Ties that gently bind,
In love, we find.
Softly woven grace,
In every warm embrace.

Underneath the skin,
Where our stories spin.
Life's tapestry unfolds,
In colors bright and bold.

Faintest echoes soar,
Yearning evermore.
Threads may fray and break,
But love is what we make.

Digital Echoes

Through the screen, I see,
Visions wild and free.
Pixels dance and play,
In a virtual way.

Echoes of our past,
In a world so vast.
Memories intertwine,
In the digital line.

Voices faintly call,
Through this endless sprawl.
Data drifts like mist,
A connection not missed.

Moments flash and fade,
In this grand parade.
Bright screens glow at night,
Revealing hidden light.

Fingers tap in haste,
Sending love, not waste.
Echoes reach afar,
Riding on a star.

Fractured Signals

Fractured whispers roam,
Searching for a home.
Signals lost in space,
Time cannot erase.

Frequency's embrace,
Echoes in this chase.
Broken lines may bend,
But they seldom end.

Static fills the air,
Waves that we must share.
Moments come and go,
In currents, they flow.

Voids filled with the sound,
Where lost dreams are found.
A melody awakes,
In the silence, shakes.

Fractured yet alive,
For connection, we strive.
In brokenness, we rise,
Finding grace in the cries.

Threads of Silence

In the stillness, shadows play,
Silent echoes drift away.
Fingers trace the empty air,
Whispers linger, quiet prayer.

Through the void, a heartbeat sounds,
Nostalgic notes the silence rounds.
Worn-out tales untold, unspent,
Each breath a gentle testament.

Veiled in dusk, secrets remain,
Silken threads of joy and pain.
In the calm, emotions swell,
Weaving dreams, a muted spell.

Beneath the weight of heavy skies,
Voices echo, soft goodbyes.
In the night, the past will weave,
Silent stories, hard to leave.

Time unwinds its fragile seam,
Life entwined in thread of dream.

Digital Echoes

In pixelated realms we roam,
Fragments of a digital home.
Voices pulse in waves of light,
Lost connections, fading bright.

Through the screen, a world unfolds,
Stories whispered, tales retold.
Threads of code that intertwine,
In this space, our hearts align.

Footprints left on virtual sand,
Touching souls we do not understand.
In this maze of endless scroll,
We search for meaning, find our role.

Frequencies shift, signals find,
Melodies that bind the mind.
Each alert a beckoning call,
In this web, we rise, we fall.

Digital dreams we chase and seek,
In silence lies the words we speak.

Fractured Signals

Waves collide in fractured space,
Lost in transmission, find the trace.
Echoes bounce from wall to wall,
In this chaos, senses stall.

Static whispers, messages blurred,
Voices rise, yet none are heard.
Fragments dance in errant light,
Shadows play, they take their flight.

Signals fade like morning mist,
In the noise, we cease to exist.
Hopes unravel, dreams split wide,
Seeking refuge where truths hide.

Frequency bends, we strain to hear,
In the silence, honesty's near.
Through the clamor, I find your name,
A beacon flickers, fuel to flame.

Fractured worlds, yet hearts can blend,
In the gaps, we comprehend.

Webs of Whispered Dreams

In the twilight, dreams take flight,
Weaving webs in soft moonlight.
Threads of magic intertwine,
Drawing hopes like stars that shine.

Each whisper carries tender grace,
Laced with warmth, a sweet embrace.
Silken strands of wish and desire,
Ignite the soul, a soft fire.

Bathed in gold, the moments glow,
With every breath, the visions flow.
A tapestry, bright and vast,
Stories from the future and past.

In the quiet, visions bloom,
Painting dreams that chase the gloom.
With every thread, a new chance seeds,
Webs crafted from our honest needs.

Within this realm, we'll softly weave,
An endless dream, together believe.

Glitches in the Infinite

In circuits wild, the whispers hum,
A cosmic dance, where errors come.
Pixels flicker, hearts entwine,
Lost in code, we seek the line.

Echoes play in binary dreams,
Fragmented thoughts, or so it seems.
In every glitch, a spark of light,
A universe born from the night.

We chase the pulse, the endless flow,
In tangled pathways, truths we sow.
Reality bends, then breaks apart,
As chaos weaves through every heart.

Yet in these faults, a beauty lies,
A tangled web beneath the skies.
Connections form in twists of fate,
Glitches define, they resonate.

Amid the noise, the silent gaze,
We find our peace in scattered ways.
Through every flaw, we come to know,
The infinite's grace, our hearts aglow.

The Art of Missing

In empty rooms where echoes play,
We brush the ghosts of yesterday.
With each reminder, moments slip,
The art of missing, a gentle grip.

Past hollow smiles, the laughter fades,
In shadows cast, the heart invades.
Dreams once bright, now veiled in gray,
The art of missing, a soft decay.

We dance in spaces yet unseen,
In memories held, we find the sheen.
Time escapes like whispers in flight,
The art of missing brings back the light.

Yet in our ache, we learn to grow,
Through every loss, love's seeds we sow.
In absence felt, connections cling,
The art of missing, the song we sing.

With open hearts, we greet the dusk,
In every void, there's fragile trust.
For in each gap, a chance to see,
The art of missing, setting us free.

Shadows of Connection

In twilight's embrace, the shadows dance,
Fleeting glimpses, a stolen chance.
Across the void, we reach in vain,
Shadows of connection, joy and pain.

Tendrils stretch in the fading light,
Silent stories, bound yet slight.
In whispered dreams, we intertwine,
Shadows of connection, yours and mine.

Through murky paths, our spirits roam,
In spaces shared, we find our home.
Yet distance lingers, a sigh, a breath,
Shadows of connection, love and death.

In each encounter, sparks ignite,
Illuminating the endless night.
Though shadows linger, hearts align,
Shadows of connection, ever divine.

We learn to dance with every ghost,
In tethered hearts, we find the most.
Together apart, our fates recline,
Shadows of connection, a sacred sign.

Tethered Yet Alone

In crowded places, silence screams,
Connections fray at the seams.
Amid the throng, we stand apart,
Tethered yet alone, a heavy heart.

Words left unspoken linger long,
In empty spaces, we feel wrong.
With every glance, our souls collide,
Yet tethered yet alone, we must hide.

Invisible threads pull us near,
Yet in our stillness, doubt and fear.
We grasp for hands that slip away,
Tethered yet alone, night and day.

Through fleeting smiles, a longing grows,
In every touch, the sadness flows.
For in our ties, there's loss and gain,
Tethered yet alone, love's bittersweet pain.

Yet hope remains in the silent throng,
In every heart, we find our song.
Though journeys weave and paths may stray,
Tethered yet alone, we'll find our way.

Networked Dreams

In the glow of screens we meet,
Whispers shared, fragile and sweet.
Threads of thought intertwine,
Creating worlds that feel divine.

In the silence, voices flow,
Echoing places we long to know.
Pixelated paths we tread,
In these dreams, our hearts are fed.

Connection blooms like wildflowers,
Growing strong in digital hours.
Every click and keystroke shared,
Ties that bind, we are ensnared.

Through webs of light, we explore,
Venturing where we've never been before.
In laughter and tears, we find a way,
In networked dreams, we dance and play.

As we wander, fears disperse,
In virtual realms, we oft immerse.
Together we're whole, though apart we seem,
In the fabric of this shared dream.

Beyond the Screen

Glimmers of light, flickering fast,
Reflections of a world amassed.
Through the glass, visions fight,
Beyond the screen, there shines a light.

Faces hidden, yet so near,
Soundless laughter, joy, and fear.
A universe in each soft glow,
Where thoughts like rivers freely flow.

Time bends here, a strange embrace,
Moments linger in this space.
Yet still we crave the touch of hands,
And find ourselves in distant lands.

With every log in, a chance to see,
Who we are and who we could be.
Beyond the screen, dreams ignite,
Creating bonds that feel so right.

Together we weave through endless night,
Crafting futures, bold and bright.
Here we are, hearts interlace,
In this realm, we find our place.

Interlinked Realities

In shadows cast by glowing light,
We roam through worlds, day and night.
Realities blend, touch and align,
In this vast expanse, hearts entwine.

What is real, what is a dream?
In every pixel, a new scheme.
Unseen threads pull us near,
In interlinked paths, we conquer fear.

Voices echo in digital streams,
Painting the world in vibrant themes.
Here we forge connections bold,
In stories shared, our lives unfold.

Waves of data, swift and true,
A tapestry woven from me and you.
In this dance, we take our stand,
Interlinked, a united band.

As we navigate this swirling sea,
We find ourselves, we set us free.
In every click, a chance to find,
A deeper link, a love intertwined.

The Web of Us

In the heart of the web, we spin,
Threads of fate where dreams begin.
Shared stories linger, strong and true,
In the fabric of love, woven me and you.

Through distant stars, our voices fly,
Connecting souls that touch the sky.
In moments fleeting, time stands still,
In the web of us, we find our will.

Here secrets dance in whispered tones,
Crafting bonds that feel like home.
Every gaze, a spark ignites,
In the web of us, the future excites.

With every heartbeat, a rhythm new,
We chart a course, explore what's true.
Together we're stronger, never alone,
In the web of us, our love has grown.

As we journey on this shared route,
Through trials faced, and joys, and doubt.
In the threads of this intricate trust,
We shine brightly, the web of us.

Frequency of Solitude

In the hush of twilight's glow,
Whispers dance, soft and slow.
Shadows stretch, like silent streams,
Carrying secrets, forgotten dreams.

A heartbeat lost in endless night,
Loneliness feels like a flight.
Each moment drips, a silent tear,
Echoing thoughts, always near.

Amidst the stars, I find my place,
A quiet breath, a gentle grace.
Time stands still, the world fades away,
In this frequency, I choose to stay.

Stillness wraps, a warm cocoon,
Finding solace in the moon.
Each sigh carries a tale untold,
Of love once cherished, now grown cold.

In solitude, I learn to see,
The art of being just me.
A melody of thoughts, profound,
In frequency, my heart is found.

Hummingbird Bridges

Wings that flutter, quick as light,
Dancing over blossoms bright.
Tiny jewels in morning's hue,
Crafting bridges old and new.

Each sip brings nectar's sweet delight,
Nature's magic, pure and right.
A moment caught, a glimpse of grace,
In every flower, a sacred space.

With iridescent glints they soar,
Across the fields, forevermore.
In the tapestry of blooms they weave,
A world where colors never leave.

Echoes of joy in the air,
Tender whispers, soft and rare.
Life's heartbeat in every flap,
Over gardens where dreams unwrap.

In moments fleeting, they remind,
To cherish what we often find.
In simple things, beauty is found,
Hummingbird bridges, love unbound.

Echoes in the Ether

Voices linger in the breeze,
Carried softly through the trees.
Memories wind like ribbons bright,
Fading gently in the night.

An unseen thread connects us all,
In whispered thoughts, we rise and fall.
Back to spaces where we belong,
In the quiet, we find our song.

Echoes ring in timeless tales,
Across the cosmos, love prevails.
Every heartbeat, every sigh,
Resonates as stars drift by.

Invisible paths we follow true,
In silent moments, we break through.
To listen deep, to understand,
The echoing song of a gentle hand.

In the ether, dreams unfold,
Carried where the stories told.
Together in this cosmic dance,
Lost and found in sweet romance.

Silence Between the Bytes

Digital pulses, fast and bright,
Yet in the chaos, finds the light.
Silence lingers, soft and near,
Between the bytes, is crystal clear.

Whispers dive in network streams,
Crafting threads of silent dreams.
In data's rush, a gentle pause,
Moments captured, just because.

Algorithms play a silent tune,
Beneath the surface, stillness bloons.
In every scroll, a breath is found,
In quiet bits, the heart's unbound.

The world can chatter, loud and bright,
But peace resides in timeless night.
In every pixel, stories weave,
Between the bytes, the soul believes.

Connections glow, though miles apart,
In wired silence, we find heart.
A moment shared, in screens we trust,
In silence between, we learn to adjust.

The Fray of Intimacy

In whispered hues, our secrets bloom,
Eclipsed by shadows, they find their room.
A dance of souls, a tangled thread,
In breaths of silence, words unsaid.

Fingertips trace the lines of fear,
A fragile bond, when you are near.
Heartbeats echo, a song of trust,
In the warmth of closeness, we find our must.

Yet storms may rise in tender tides,
As whispered dreams turn into rides.
Intimacy's fray shows paths untrod,
In tangled webs, we search for God.

Behind the walls, the laughter fades,
Beneath the mask, a heart parades.
The tender ache of love's embrace,
In the fray of intimacy, we find our place.

And as we stand in this shared space,
With every challenge, a new trace.
Woven together, we are one,
In the fray, our journey's begun.

Luminous Silences

In the hushed night, the stars align,
Whispers of light through the shadows shine.
Each pause a shimmer, soft and bright,
Luminous silences cast a warm light.

Breath held close, a moment freezes,
Within the quiet, understanding pleases.
The heart speaks volumes, unspoken grace,
In luminous silences, we find our place.

Glimmers of thought in twilight's hold,
Like molten silver, they shimmer gold.
Echoes of love, a sacred art,
In silence, we stitch together our heart.

Vows unvoiced, yet deeply felt,
Fragments of dreams in stillness melt.
In random moments, truth ignites,
In luminous silences, we find our heights.

No need for words, just starry night,
In the calm embrace, everything feels right.
Together we wander, hand in hand,
In luminous silences, we understand.

Voices Amidst the Static

Amidst the noise, a whisper grows,
Voices break through, soft and low.
In the chaos, a melody stands,
A song of hope in trembling hands.

Frequency shifts in the dusk of dreams,
Echoes of truth flicker in beams.
When shadows merge with gleaming light,
Voices emerge, a powerful sight.

Through the static, we seek the clear,
A battle cry, a call sincere.
Harmonies rise, the silence divides,
In the noise, our courage resides.

Every note a promise made,
A tapestry of truths conveyed.
Hope lingers softly, piercing the night,
Voices amidst the static, shining bright.

Together we weave, in colors vast,
In the tumult, we hold steadfast.
With every heartbeat, a resonant track,
Voices amidst the static, we won't look back.

Boundaries of Emotion

In the depths of hearts, a line is drawn,
A fragile border, dusk to dawn.
Where love can flourish or fears will grow,
In boundaries of emotion, we often sow.

Tender feelings can shift like sand,
A boundary shifts as we take a stand.
With every tear, a lesson learned,
In the fire of passion, our souls are burned.

The dance of joy, the ache of pain,
In boundaries crossed, we lose and gain.
With fragile hearts, we wade through hues,
In boundaries of emotion, we choose to lose.

Each moment shared, a step we take,
In the dance of love, our hearts awake.
Through laughter echoes, through vibrant cries,
In boundaries of emotion, our spirit flies.

So let us tread with care and grace,
In this tender realm, we find our space.
Through joy and sorrow, we move to blend,
In boundaries of emotion, love knows no end.

Untangling the Noise

Amidst the clamor, I seek the calm,
Voices fade, like a distant psalm.
Thoughts intertwine, a tangled thread,
Yearning for peace, where silence is spread.

Whispers echo in the crowded space,
Chasing shadows, I find my place.
In the mist of chatter, I hold my ground,
Listening close, for the sweet sound.

Fading echoes make way for light,
Notes of clarity, sparkling bright.
Moving through layers, I shed the fray,
Finding the truth that guides my way.

Rustling leaves, a gentle embrace,
Nature speaks in a tender grace.
Untangling the threads, I weave a tune,
In stillness, I find my heart's warm boon.

Here in the quiet, I craft my dreams,
Cleansing the noise, or so it seems.
With every breath, I reclaim my voice,
In a world of chaos, I make my choice.

Shadows of Unsaid

In the silence where secrets dwell,
Words unspoken, a quiet spell.
Lingering thoughts, beneath the skin,
Echoes of doubts that might have been.

Eyes meet briefly, stories unfold,
In every glance, a truth untold.
Bridges imagined, yet never crossed,
In the shadows, our lives get lost.

Whispers dangle in the air we share,
Heavy with meaning, a weight to bear.
Moments stolen, they drift like smoke,
Building a wall with each silent yoke.

Through the twilight, we navigate fear,
With every heartbeat, I wish you near.
The shadows linger, but hope remains,
In the dance of words, love breaks the chains.

Together in silence, we forge a way,
Trusting the feelings that words can't say.
In shadows of unsaid, we find our light,
Illuminating bonds, strong and bright.

Amongst the Waves

Beneath the ocean's vast embrace,
Tides pulling gently, a rhythmic pace.
Waves whisper softly, tales of old,
In their crests, mysteries unfold.

Shells scatter secrets on sandy shores,
Crashing a melody, nature's scores.
The sun dips low, casting golden rays,
Amongst the waves, the heart plays.

Salty breezes wrap around my soul,
A dance with the tides, I feel whole.
Every surge, a chance to connect,
The ebbing flow, a sweet effect.

Stars twinkle above in velvet nights,
Guiding the dreamers, igniting lights.
Amongst the waves, where wishes soar,
I find my peace upon the shore.

Nature's rhythm, a timeless song,
In the orchestra of tides, I belong.
Where currents intertwine, love finds a place,
Amongst the waves, I embrace the grace.

Connected by Quiet

In the stillness, our hearts align,
Where silence blooms, and the stars shine.
Hands held gently, a knowing glance,
Connected by quiet, we take our chance.

Amidst the noise, we find our way,
In whispered dreams, our spirits sway.
Moments linger, time slows its race,
In the quietude, we carve our space.

The world fades, just you and I,
Lost in the glimmers of a soft sigh.
Each pause between us, a sacred thread,
In the quiet, our essence is fed.

Harmony dances in the hush we share,
Every heartbeat takes us there.
In the absence of chaos, love ignites,
Connected by quiet, we reach new heights.

As shadows lengthen, we draw near,
In the silence, I hold you dear.
Together we wander, hearts intertwined,
In the calm of the night, our souls combined.

Echoes of Absence

In the silence where voices fade,
Whispers linger, memories made.
Shadows dance where light once played,
Echoes of you, forever invade.

Time drifts softly, like a breeze,
Moments caught in distant freeze.
Each thought of you bends like trees,
In the heart, a longing disease.

The clock ticks slowly, marking pain,
Each second draws me back again.
In every laugh, I hear your name,
A ghost that sparks a tender flame.

With every sunset, colors blend,
Nature's palette, hearts transcend.
Yet in the night, I cannot mend,
The silent void where dreams suspend.

So close, yet miles away it seems,
Reality shatters all my dreams.
Yet hope persists in silver beams,
As absence weaves through fragile seams.

Conversations Untethered

Words float free like autumn leaves,
Drifting gently, no one grieves.
Through the air, unanchored pleas,
Yearning hearts find paths to ease.

Thoughts collide in spaces vast,
Moments shared that slip so fast.
In this dance, none unsurpassed,
Fleeting echoes of the past.

A laughter shared on a winding road,
Secrets whispered, stories flowed.
Every silence, a heavy load,
Yet truth is light, and love bestowed.

In these chats where souls ignite,
Connection blooms in darkest night.
Every glance a spark of light,
In the chaos, hearts take flight.

Yet words unsaid can weigh us down,
An untold tale in every town.
Conversations, lost and found,
In shared stories, we're unbound.

In the Space Between

Between the stars, a soft embrace,
Silent wishes find their place.
In the quiet, we trace the grace,
Of fleeting moments, time's own face.

A heartbeat echoes, poised and low,
In the silence, feelings grow.
Every pause, a chance to know,
In the stillness, love's gentle flow.

The spaces linger, weigh on dreams,
Filled with questions, hope redeems.
Through the shadows, soft light gleams,
In the gaps, are scattered beams.

Between the whispers, secrets hide,
In the void, our truths reside.
Through the dark, we must decide,
To bridge the chasm, side by side.

And so we dance in quiet grace,
In the space where souls embrace.
Every heartbeat, a warm trace,
In the silence, we find our place.

Threads of Irony

In tangled webs of fate we weave,
Dreams and truths that both deceive.
A smile masks the pain we grieve,
In the irony, hearts believe.

Promises made in fleeting light,
Often turn to shadows bright.
In the silence of the night,
Truths are lost, yet spirits fight.

We chase the dawn, as shadows loom,
Painting joy, despite the gloom.
Yet through the chaos, seeds can bloom,
Irony crafts a hopeful room.

Conversations wrapped in playful jest,
Hide the weight that haunts our quest.
Yet in the laughter, we find rest,
In irony's arms, we are blessed.

So dance along this twisted thread,
With every word, let courage spread.
Embrace the paradox instead,
For in the irony, love is fed.

Networks of the Heart

In whispers soft as twilight's glow,
Connections start to ebb and flow.
A pulse that beats beyond the skin,
Where love and hope begin within.

Threads weave tight in silent threads,
We dance on paths our hearts have led.
Each spark ignites a fire anew,
Lighting the dark with shades of blue.

Through laughter shared and tears we shed,
In realms of trust, our spirits spread.
From every glance, the tales unfold,
In networks strong, our stories told.

Like constellations in the night,
Our journeys blend, a shared delight.
Each heart a node, so brightly shines,
Entwined in love's electric lines.

In moments brief, yet deeply felt,
The warmth of friendship softly melts.
In networks vast, we find our art,
Creating worlds within the heart.

Longing in an Instant

A glance exchanged, the world holds breath,
In silence thick, love dances death.
Within that gleam, all time suspends,
A fleeting dream that never ends.

The rush of heartbeats, a stolen sight,
In crowded rooms, we feel the light.
Yet shadows linger, haunting space,
As longing paints each passing face.

In every sigh, a wish takes flight,
On whispered winds through starry night.
A moment clenched, so pure, so rare,
Yet slips away like fleeting air.

The clock ticks soft, yet loud it seems,
In every pause, we weave our dreams.
A split second, worlds collide,
Bound by the pull of love and pride.

In every heartbeat, echoes rise,
A thousand words within the eyes.
For every instant, long we yearn,
To capture time, to feel Love's burn.

Between Us: A Static Silence

Words unspoken, heavy in the air,
A quiet void, yet we both stare.
Invisible threads stretch far apart,
Between the silence, beats the heart.

Fingers brush, a tension grows,
In this stillness, the feeling flows.
What lies beneath the silent space?
An aching need, a warm embrace.

Every heartbeat marks the time,
In static pulse, we read the rhyme.
Yet courage falters in the night,
As shadows loom, obscuring light.

Our eyes may meet, yet words retreat,
In whispered dreams, our souls repeat.
Though silence speaks, it cannot tell,
The depth of love that binds us well.

Between us lies a world untold,
In every gaze, a story bold.
Yet still, we linger, hushed and tense,
In static silence, love's suspense.

The Spaces We Don't Fill

Each empty chair speaks volumes loud,
In spaces left, we move the crowd.
The echoes of what once was here,
Throb softly, whispering our fear.

In shadows cast, memories blend,
A tapestry that has no end.
Each laugh we shared, each tear we cried,
Now haunt the space where love once thrived.

Unspoken words float in the air,
Building walls we thought were rare.
In every pause, a thought distills,
Of all the spaces we don't fill.

With every dawn, new light unveils,
The love that lingers, still prevails.
Yet in that gap, the heart does sigh,
For what remains, it asks us why.

So here we sit, in quiet grace,
Facing the void, our tender space.
In every gap, we find it clear,
The spaces left bind us near.

Nodes of Emotion

Silent whispers in the night,
Echoes of a heart's delight.
Moments tethered, feelings shared,
In the warmth of hope, we dared.

Fragile threads of laughter spun,
Woven deep with each new sun.
Lingering dreams that break the mold,
Painted skies of red and gold.

Tidal waves of joy and pain,
Mysteries that we can't explain.
Subtle shifts in every glance,
Life's responses in a dance.

In the chaos, we still find,
A tender hand, a loving mind.
Through the storm, we hold on tight,
Guided by the stars at night.

Together we create our lore,
Every heartbeat, something more.
Nodes of love, we intertwine,
Forever seeking the divine.

Interwoven Journeys

Threads that stretch from heart to heart,
Each step taken, a brand new start.
Colors blend in vibrant hue,
Crafting tales both old and new.

Winding roads beneath our feet,
Carrying dreams, our souls to meet.
With every turn, we learn to grow,
Friendships bloom like flowers in snow.

Underneath the same vast sky,
Whispers carry thoughts that fly.
Mirrored paths and gentle signs,
Fates entwined like climbing vines.

Every challenge builds our grace,
In this uncharted, sacred space.
Step by step, we find our way,
Hand in hand, come what may.

Across the distance, love will call,
Interwoven, we won't fall.
In the journey, we discover,
The beauty found in every other.

Circuitous Paths

Winding roads without a plan,
Every choice, a shift in sand.
Lost and found in twists and turns,
With each step, a lesson learned.

Every corner holds a tale,
Where hearts beat and hopes set sail.
Through the shadows, light will seep,
Guiding us to promises we keep.

In the maze of life we roam,
Seeking solace, finding home.
Every challenge, we embrace,
In the journey, we find grace.

Hands will reach from dark to light,
Leading voices through the night.
Paths converge, and destinies blend,
In the silence, we ascend.

With each leap, we redefine,
Trusting in the grand design.
In the circuit, we connect,
Every heart, a new project.

Disconnect to Connect

In the silence, voices fade,
Invisible walls slowly made.
Yet in stillness, truths arise,
Breaking chains, we claim the skies.

Unraveled threads we gently weave,
Fractured paths we dare to leave.
In the chaos, light will spark,
Illuminating every dark.

From disconnect, we start to see,
The power found in empathy.
Bridges built from heart to heart,
Together we create our art.

Through the gaps, we find our voice,
In the quiet, we rejoice.
Spaces filled with hope's embrace,
Finding love in every place.

Let the shadows fade away,
In the dawn, we find our way.
From disconnect, the ties reflect,
In the light, we reconnect.

Transmissions of Longing

Across the twilight sky, we send our dreams,
Whispers carried on soft, fading beams.
Every heartbeat echoes, a distant call,
In the silence, we feel the longing thrall.

Stars shine brightly, painting the night,
Guiding our souls with flickering light.
Yearning for moments we dare not speak,
In the darkness, it's connection we seek.

Messages linger in the space in-between,
Threads of hope woven through the unseen.
In the void, we find what we desire,
Fueling our hearts with an unquenchable fire.

The sky becomes a canvas to our fate,
As our hopes ascend, we contemplate.
With each transmission, we build a bridge,
Across the chasm, on a fragile ridge.

In the stillness, we find our resolve,
In quiet moments, our spirits evolve.
Transmissions of longing, forever entwined,
In the vast expanse, our hearts aligned.

Fading Frequencies

In the distance, a signal starts to wane,
Echoes of laughter slowly turn to pain.
As the night grows old, the whispers fade,
Leaving behind a promise unmade.

Once vibrant voices in a wild dance,
Now mere shadows that never had a chance.
The air is thick with what was once clear,
Fading frequencies that no one can hear.

Memories flicker like stars in decline,
Haunted by moments that felt so divine.
Each heartbeat a reminder of lost refrain,
As silence envelops the remnants of gain.

We search for a signal, a trace of the past,
In the echoes of time, we hope it will last.
Yet the more we reach out, the more we lose hold,
Fading frequencies, stories untold.

But in the quiet, we learn to embrace,
The beauty in loss, the truth in our space.
Though the music may fade, the notes remain,
Fading frequencies, our hearts still sustain.

The Weight of Unsaid Words

In the silence, secrets begin to grow,
Words take on weight, a heavy shadow.
Every glance exchanged, a story suppressed,
The weight of unsaid words leaves us stressed.

Thoughts jostle in corners, yearning to find,
A way to escape and unravel the mind.
Each pause stretches long, like an endless sea,
The weight of unsaid words binding you and me.

We dance around meanings, hints left unspun,
With fear of the storm that might come undone.
In the echo of silence, tension resides,
The weight of unsaid words, love that collides.

Yet in vulnerability lies the key,
To free the heart, to set it all free.
Breaking the silence, we'll find our way,
Unsaid words become light, come what may.

Together we'll gather the fragments we've lost,
Courageous and bold, unafraid of the cost.
For the weight of unsaid words can transform,
Into a symphony, a new love reborn.

Cartwheeling through the Ether

Spinning through space, we find our delight,
Cartwheeling freely into the night.
With arms wide open, we embrace the unknown,
Each movement a story, a dream newly sown.

The stars become partners in our wild dance,
Guiding our hearts, giving love a chance.
In the cosmic ballet, we twirl and we sway,
Cartwheeling through the ether, come what may.

With laughter like music and joy in our souls,
We leap through the void, daring to be whole.
In a dance with the universe, we find our true place,
Cartwheeling gently, drifting through space.

Chaos and beauty entwined in each turn,
In the fire of starlight, our spirits will burn.
With every rotation, we shed what we know,
Cartwheeling through the ether, ever aglow.

So let go of fears, let the magic ignite,
Join in the rhythm, embrace the flight.
For in cartwheeling joy, we are forever free,
Dancing through time, just you and me.

Disconnecting Bridges

Once we stood on a bridge of dreams,
Now the distance stretches wide,
Words like whispers fall apart,
Echoes of love secretly hide.

Time drifts like leaves in the wind,
Familiar paths we used to tread,
Silent moments fill the space,
In the silence, we're misled.

Bridges crumble, stones erode,
Paths we walked lost to the night,
Hearts once close, now fade from view,
In the shadows, there's no light.

We built our towers with trust and hope,
Now they stand in disrepair,
The distance grows like a canyon wide,
As we struggle to breathe the air.

What once was shared is now a dream,
A distant memory, a faded song,
Disconnecting bridges, we drift apart,
Two souls lost where they don't belong.

Conversations in the Void

Whispers linger in empty space,
Words unspoken touch the skin,
In the quiet, thoughts collide,
Lost in silence, we begin.

Voices echo without a sound,
Messages trapped in the night,
Loneliness wraps like a shroud,
Dreams flicker, just out of sight.

Fingers reach for what's unseen,
Connections sought but never found,
In the void, we chase our dreams,
As the shadows swirl around.

Particles dance in endless grace,
Building bridges across the dark,
Conversations without a face,
Yet still we reach with a spark.

In this vast and empty space,
We find solace in shared thought,
As the universe watches close,
Within the void, we are caught.

Shadows of a Click

In the glow of the screen we meet,
Pixels flashing, hearts aflame,
Shadows flicker with each small breath,
In this world, we're not the same.

A click connects, a moment shared,
Yet deeper ties remain unseen,
Voices trapped within the code,
Searching for what might have been.

Fingers dance on a cold keyboard,
Thoughts spill out into the night,
Shadows paint our conversations,
As we chase the glowing light.

Echoes linger after each sound,
Tangled webs of dreams and fear,
In the shadows, we'll find our truth,
Though the distance feels so near.

Together apart, we play our roles,
Craving more than just a spark,
In the shadows of a click,
Our hearts ignite, leaving a mark.

Unseen Connections

Invisible threads tie us close,
Though miles may stand in our way,
Hearts beat strong in harmony,
Singing softly, night and day.

In silence, we understand,
A bond that transcends all space,
Like starlight across the cosmos,
A gentle touch, a warm embrace.

Words unspoken, yet we feel,
The pull of an unseen thread,
Like a whisper in the dark,
Guiding us, lightening the dread.

In moments shared and memories made,
Connections form beneath the skin,
Though we may wander far apart,
In our hearts, the ties begin.

Unseen connections present and true,
We are more than what we see,
Bound by love, divided by time,
Forever more, you're part of me.

Veins of Cybernetic Life

In circuits hum the whispers bright,
A dance of data in the night.
The pulse of wires, electric streams,
Breathes life into our waking dreams.

Through glass and steel, our thoughts collide,
In cyber realms where hopes abide.
With every keystroke, worlds unfold,
A tapestry of futures bold.

Neon veins, they intertwine,
In digital gardens where we shine.
The heartbeats sync, a syncopated sound,
In cyberspace, our souls are found.

Yet wires can cut and break apart,
A fracture blooms within the heart.
In shadows cast by glowing screens,
We seek the warmth of silent means.

As pixels fade, we search for grace,
In tangled webs, we find our place.
In veins of life, both real and dreamed,
A symphony of love redeemed.

Shared Spaces, Divided Souls

In crowded rooms, we stand apart,
Two vessels filled, yet not one heart.
With laughter loud, we bridge the gap,
Still craving comfort in our trap.

Familiar faces, eyes that stray,
In silent whispers, words decay.
We walk the line of who we need,
In shared spaces, our souls proceed.

Unseen barriers rise with grace,
These walls divide, yet time can't erase.
Lingering glances say it all,
In fleeting moments, we rise and fall.

Yet in the void of night's embrace,
We yearn for warmth in every trace.
Our hearts entwined, though miles apart,
In shared spaces, we find our art.

So here we stand, both near and far,
In this paradox, our guiding star.
Divided souls, yet joined as one,
In the dance of life, we come undone.

Interference of the Heart

A static hum fills silent air,
When heartbeats clash, we feel the scare.
With every glance, a signal lost,
We navigate the tangled frost.

In tender moments, words betray,
The frequency gets drowned in gray.
A thunderstorm of hopes collides,
Emotions echo, love abides.

In quiet spaces, shivers run,
Interference blurs what's just begun.
Yet through the noise, a whisper calls,
In tangled thoughts, our courage falls.

So let us tune to loving sounds,
Find harmony in whispered rounds.
In every heartbeat, a glimpse of light,
Guiding us back from endless night.

For though the static may confound,
Our hearts still sing, a perfect sound.
Through interference, we'll find our way,
In love's embrace, forever stay.

When Lines are Drawn

In dusty halls, we stake our claim,
With words like swords, we draw our fame.
Lines are drawn in shifting sand,
Dividing paths, we take a stand.

A sudden silence fills the air,
As tensions rise, we find despair.
But still, we reach across the line,
Though shadows linger, hearts align.

We stand in colors, bold and bright,
Yet fear the clash between wrong and right.
In every breath, a choice remains,
To cross the lines or bear the chains.

In battles fought, we learn to grow,
Through every conflict, love will show.
When lines are drawn, we must decide,
To bridge the gaps or run and hide.

With courage deep, we face the flame,
For in the end, it's love we name.
When lines are drawn, let kindness reign,
And from the strife, we rise again.

Frayed Connections

In crowded rooms, we lose our names,
Echoed laughter, yet none remain.
Fingers touch, yet hearts drift wide,
In silence, secrets we abide.

Beneath the weight of tangled wires,
We search for warmth amidst the fires.
Ghosts of friendships linger near,
While shadows dance and disappear.

With every call that goes unmet,
We weave the webs of our regret.
Yet hope glimmers, a distant star,
Reminding us just who we are.

The past hangs heavy, threads unspun,
In faded photos, stories run.
But somewhere deep in the night's embrace,
Frayed connections still find their place.

So here we stand, with hearts exposed,
Navigating paths no one knows.
A journey forged in tangled ways,
We rise again to greet the day.

Love in the Time of Algorithms

Swiping right on fractured dreams,
In pixelated love, it seems.
Hearts that race with every ping,
The spark of hope, a digital fling.

Data points in silent spheres,
Tracking joy, but not the tears.
In coded lines, affection hides,
While real emotions slip and slide.

Algorithm spins, it knows our ways,
Yet fails to grasp our messy days.
Love is more than ones and zeros,
It's laughter shared, it's warmth in heroes.

Moments lost in endless scrolls,
While longing pulses in our souls.
Can we break free from this charade?
Or are we trapped in the games we've played?

Still, through screens, a spark ignites,
Two souls connecting, hearts take flight.
Beyond the code, a truth will shine,
Love echoes loud, both yours and mine.

The Art of Unseen Bonds

Threads of silence weave our fate,
A glance exchanged, no need to state.
In crowded moments, hearts aligned,
A sacred pact, often confined.

Beneath the noise, a gentle hum,
A language shared by those who come.
Ties crafted in the quiet space,
Where words dissolve, and hearts embrace.

With every heartbeat, shadows play,
A tether formed in dusk and day.
Not bound by sight, yet deeply felt,
Invisible strings, expertly dealt.

In laughter's echo, we entwine,
Painting a canvas so divine.
Though worlds apart, together stand,
The art of unseen bonds is grand.

So when the storms of life arise,
And distance stretches across the skies,
Remember, in the quiet, strong,
Unseen bonds, where we belong.

Flickering Lights

Stars above, they blink and fade,
Whispers of a serenade.
In the darkness, dreams ignite,
Dance like fireflies in the night.

A single flame can spark a blaze,
Illuminating hidden ways.
In corners dim, where shadows play,
Flickering lights will lead the way.

When hope feels lost in endless maze,
Catch the glow of fleeting rays.
In fragile moments, truths unfold,
Flickering lights, a story told.

Through silence soft, the heart will call,
In tender glows, we rise, we fall.
With every flicker, a breath anew,
Shining bright, in shades of blue.

So let us cherish each small spark,
In the depths of the merciless dark.
For in the night, we find our sight,
In flickering lights, we chase the light.

Echoing Solitudes

In the silence of the night,
Whispers dance with the light.
Lonely stars in a velvet sky,
Echoes fade as time drifts by.

Shadows merge with the dawn,
Fleeting dreams that are gone.
Hearts beat in quiet refrain,
Solitudes whisper the pain.

Silent footsteps on the ground,
In the void, no solace found.
Yet in solitude, we grow,
In the echoes, love will glow.

Beneath the moon's gentle gaze,
Lost in a forgotten haze.
Nature speaks in tones so clear,
Solitudes draw ever near.

In the vastness, we remain,
Stillness wraps like a chain.
Caught in cycles, we abide,
In the echoes, dreams collide.

Bridges Built on Air

Between two worlds, a thought,
A fragile bond that we sought.
With every whisper, we dare,
Building bridges that are rare.

Clouds of dreams drift high above,
Carried by the strength of love.
In our hands, we hold the threads,
Tying hearts as silence spreads.

Moments flicker like a flame,
Each connection, not the same.
Through the mist, we reach, we try,
Crafting paths that span the sky.

In the space between two minds,
Magic lingers, love unwinds.
With every heartbeat, we soar,
Through the air, we yearn for more.

Hold my hand, we'll float away,
In this dance, we learn to play.
Every glance a step we take,
On the air, our dreams awake.

Conundrums of Togetherness

In the tapestry of time,
Threads of hope intertwine.
With every moment we spend,
Conundrums never end.

Laughter echoes in the storm,
Hearts collide, a brand-new form.
In the chaos, we find peace,
A fleeting, sweet release.

Questions linger in the air,
Binding souls with a prayer.
In the silence, we reflect,
On the love that we protect.

Together, yet so far apart,
Each step, a beating heart.
In the maze, we share our fears,
Woven deep through joy and tears.

Moments shining like a star,
In this life, we've come so far.
Togetherness, a riddle bold,
In each other, we find gold.

Paths entwined, we march ahead,
With every word left unsaid.
In the puzzle, love will guide,
Through the storms, we will reside.

The Distance of a Key Stroke

Fingers dance on keys so light,
Words emerge, take graceful flight.
In the stillness of the night,
Messages forge bonds so tight.

Miles apart, yet close we feel,
Through the screen, the heart reveals.
Every letter, pulse and beat,
Across the void, we find our seat.

In the hum of circuits' whine,
Longing whispers, yours and mine.
Every text a bridge we build,
In the silence, love fulfilled.

In the glow of a gentle screen,
Dreams are shared and hearts convene.
With each press, a world unfolds,
In the distance, love retolds.

Time dissolves in pixel's grace,
Finding home in this space.
With a keystroke, we transcend,
In the ether, moments blend.

Though the world may seem so vast,
In our words, we hold steadfast.
Distance fades with every line,
In this dance, your hand in mine.

Ties that Bind, Yet Break

In shadows cast by whispers low,
Threads of love can twist and bow.
Promises made in the light,
Fade to silence in the night.

Hearts entwined in a gentle dance,
Fate's cruel hand seizes the chance.
What once was strong begins to fray,
In this game, we lose our way.

Dreams are woven with sweet intent,
Yet through time, the fabric's spent.
Unraveled hopes lay on the floor,
Echoes of what was before.

Ties that bind can feel so tight,
Yet break apart without a fight.
The struggle to hold on is real,
But what remains is hard to feel.

In the end, through joy and strife,
We find the lessons of our life.
Though ties may break, we must be bold,
For new beginnings can unfold.

Waves of Isolation

In a sea of voices all around,
A lonely heart cannot be found.
Crashing waves off distant shores,
Echoing silence, the spirit roars.

Drifting thoughts like paper boats,
Caught in currents, lost in notes.
Yearning for a hand to hold,
In the depths, the stories told.

An ocean wide, yet worlds apart,
We sail alone, without a chart.
The tides bring shadows, dark and deep,
In the stillness, our sorrows seep.

But in the dark, stars flicker bright,
Guiding souls through the long night.
With every wave that pulls us down,
We rise again, no time to drown.

In isolation, we learn to grow,
Embracing winds that once felt slow.
For in the vastness, hope takes flight,
Waves of isolation lead to light.

Interwoven Paths

In the tapestry of life we tread,
Every choice a thread we've bred.
Paths that cross, then fade away,
Leaving marks on hearts that stay.

Moments shared in laughter's glow,
Intertwined like roots below.
Fates entwined in silent grace,
As we journey to find our place.

Winding roads may break apart,
Yet the echoes hold the heart.
Each encounter, a gentle thread,
Stitching love where pain once led.

Weaving dreams on a loom of time,
Life's patterns shift, they twist, they climb.
In every turn, a lesson learned,
As the fires of passion burned.

Though some may wander, lose their way,
Others find their home, they stay.
In every thread and every seam,
Interwoven paths fulfill the dream.

Fragments of a Virtual Heart

In the glow of screens, we reside,
Sharing thoughts we cannot hide.
Pixels dance, a digital art,
Yet loneliness fills the virtual heart.

Messages flow like fleeting dreams,
Connections made, or so it seems.
Fractured whispers, truths untold,
Behind each smile, a tear of gold.

In this realm of electric breath,
We chase the shadows, fear the depth.
But in the fragments, lives collide,
As we long for someone to confide.

Yet in the chaos, hope remains,
A light that sparks amidst the chains.
With every click, a soft embrace,
Fractured hearts can find their place.

Though distance separates our souls,
Virtual threads can make us whole.
In fragments shared, a love can start,
As we mend our virtual heart.

Screenlit Shadows

In the glow of the night, we connect,
Fingers dance on glass, moments reflect.
Whispers of souls, in pixels they blend,
Yet shadows remain, with time we transcend.

Lost in the light, are we truly awake?
Through screens we reach, but what do we make?
Conversations crude, in brevity stand,
Yet longing for warmth, to truly understand.

Stories unfold in a flickering hue,
Fleeting encounters, just me and you.
Every notification, a heartbeat's call,
Yet in all the noise, will we hear it at all?

Screens may embrace us, but hearts still yearn,
For gentle voices and smiles that burn.
As shadows move with the dimming light,
We seek the real, through the endless night.

So let's step away from this glowing sphere,
Find solace in silence, together, my dear.
In nature's embrace, let our spirits roam,
For it's in the shadows we find our true home.

Tethered Hearts

In the woven threads of fate we find,
Hearts entwined softly, together aligned.
Each heartbeat echoes, a song in the dark,
In this dance of life, you ignite the spark.

Through trials we forge, with laughter and tears,
Understanding grows, calming our fears.
With tethered souls, we face the unknown,
In every moment, a love brightly shown.

Hands clasped tightly, we weather the storm,
Finding our solace, in each other's warmth.
In the silence shared, our spirits ignite,
Tethered together, we take on the night.

Through valleys of doubt, we bravely traverse,
In the pages of life, our story's diverse.
Each chapter unfolds, with lessons to learn,
In the glow of our love, forever we burn.

So let us gather these moments we share,
With open hearts, in this journey laid bare.
For with every heartbeat, we whisper our dreams,
Tethered together, we're stronger than seams.

Signals Lost at Sea

Amidst the vast waves, the echoes fade,
Tangled in currents, our hopes evade.
Lost in the fog, where silence prevails,
We chase the horizon, as courage wails.

The lighthouse dimmed, our guide turned away,
Searching for meaning in the break of day.
Every signal sent, but the answers are few,
Adrift in the twilight, just me and the blue.

Stars once adorned, now hidden from sight,
In the depth of the ocean, we tread through the night.
With tempests surrounding, our dreams drift apart,
Yet deep in the tide, beats a resilient heart.

The horizon whispers, of lands yet to roam,
In the waves' gentle embrace, we start to feel home.
In the chaos of waters, new life can begin,
For sometimes in loss, the journey leads in.

So we set our course, through the swirling gray,
With each passing wave, we learn to sway.
For even lost signals may find their own way,
In the journey of hearts, come what may.

Between the Lines of Code

In the realm of zeros, in the one's embrace,
Logic and chaos find their own place.
Between the lines where the language flows,
Dreams intertwine as the rhythm grows.

Syntax and symbols, a digital dance,
Crafting our futures, with lines of chance.
In the depths of a program, emotions reside,
Between the commands, our feelings can hide.

As algorithms shift, narratives form,
Inside the matrix, we weather the storm.
Yet beneath the surface, connections may bloom,
Words unspoken, give voice to the room.

In the heartbeat of circuits, we sculpt our art,
Translating our passion, each line plays a part.
With every debug, our vision refined,
Between the errors, true solace we find.

So let us explore this expansive terrain,
Where dreams take flight, where love won't wane.
For between the lines of code lies our fate,
In every creation, we resonate.

Wireless Yearnings

In the quiet hum of night,
I search for signals of your light.
Connections fade, yet dreams remain,
Whispers of love in joyful pain.

A dance of stars within my mind,
Each pulse a memory we find.
Longing lingers in the air,
A silent promise, always there.

Echoes of laughter intertwine,
In the void, our hearts align.
Waves of warmth through distant views,
In every pulse, I feel you choose.

Threads of hope weave through the dark,
In every shadow, there's a spark.
Messages sent from heart to heart,
In this wireless world, we're never apart.

As dawn breaks through the heavy haze,
Longing deepens in the morning rays.
Though miles separate, love is bold,
In wireless yearnings, we grow old.

Unwritten Letters in a Digital Sky

In the glow of screens at night,
Words unspoken take their flight.
Each moment lives, a thought unshared,
In digital silence, dreams are bared.

The cosmic canvas calls your name,
A tapestry of love untamed.
Unwritten letters float on high,
In every star, our hopes reside.

To pen a word, to bridge the gap,
Yet time slips through like fleeting sap.
These silent pages wait in vain,
For ink to flow from love's refrain.

We wander through this world online,
In hidden corners, hearts entwine.
Yet real connection longs to be,
More than just a message sent free.

So in this digital expanse wide,
Let's meet beyond these waves of tide.
In whispered dreams and hopeful sighs,
Unwritten letters in a digital sky.

Virtual Embrace

In the glow of pixels bright,
I feel your warmth, a soft invite.
Virtual arms reach out in space,
In coded dreams, I find your grace.

Through screens of glass, our spirits blend,
In every chat, you are my friend.
A heartbeat echoes, faint yet clear,
In this realm, you're always near.

Yet touch eludes our longing souls,
A distance feels like bitter coals.
Still, laughter shines through every byte,
In virtual realms, we chase the light.

Fragments of love in messages sent,
Our hearts dance on in sweet content.
Just one more click, and we unite,
In every pixel, you feel so right.

So here we stand, in worlds apart,
Yet you have claimed a space in my heart.
In virtual embrace, we softly sway,
Love knows no bounds, come what may.

Real Echo

In the quiet, I hear your name,
A real echo, whispering flames.
The world shifts, yet time feels still,
In this moment, I feel your will.

No filters hide the truth we share,
In your essence, I breathe the air.
Fleeting seconds turn into dreams,
With every glance, love gently beams.

We chase the stars across the night,
In real echoes, we find our light.
Your laughter dances in the breeze,
Bringing warmth, putting my heart at ease.

Though miles apart and time unkind,
Your spirit's presence, I still find.
Together in this space we roam,
An echo that always feels like home.

So let's embrace the magic here,
In every glance, you reappear.
Real echoes linger, always true,
In this vast world, it's me and you.

Conduits of Longing

Through wires thick and signals thin,
We find the ways to let love in.
Conduits flowing, spirits entwined,
Distance shortens, hearts aligned.

In every message, a soft caress,
In longing's depth, we find our bliss.
The currents pulse with every sigh,
Together we rise, together we fly.

Love travels fast on waves we ride,
In this journey, you're by my side.
Each word a bridge, each glance a key,
Unlocking dreams, setting us free.

Across the miles, our hearts connect,
In conduits strong, we find respect.
No space too vast, no void too wide,
In our longing, forever abide.

As night unfolds with stars aglow,
Our love becomes the warmth we know.
Through conduits forged in fire and light,
Together we dance, in love's sweet flight.

Heartbeats Across the Abyss

In shadows cast by silent night,
A pulse resounds, a distant light.
Two souls entwined, yet far apart,
Their yearnings echo in the heart.

With every breath, the void does sing,
Of hopes and dreams that love can bring.
Through darkness thick, a thread so fine,
It binds their hearts, a sacred line.

Across the chasm, whispers soar,
A promise kept, forever more.
Though miles may stretch and time may bend,
Their heartbeats share, they never end.

In silent screams, the night unfolds,
A tapestry of tales retold.
With every beat, they bridge the space,
In love's embrace, they find their place.

Together strong, though worlds apart,
Two heartbeats dance, a work of art.
Through the abyss, they rise above,
United still, in endless love.

Whispers in a Digital Storm

Fingers type with frantic speed,
In pixels bright, our hearts we plead.
Across the wires, we share our thoughts,
In a digital storm, connection's sought.

Echoes bounce from screen to screen,
In fragile light, emotions glean.
A whispered laugh, a silent tear,
In coded lines, we draw near.

Amidst the chaos, still we find,
A thread of hope, forever entwined.
Every message a bridge we build,
In bytes and bits, our souls fulfilled.

But storms can rage and tempests rise,
A fleeting glitch, a sweet surprise.
In static noise, our hearts can crash,
Yet in the silence, sparks still flash.

Together we stand, despite the storm,
In digital realms, our spirits warm.
From scattered signals, love takes flight,
In whispers soft, we find our light.

Cascading Connections

Through falling leaves, the whispers flow,
A network formed where feelings grow.
In shared glances, a spark ignites,
Cascading joy in soft moonlight.

With every step, we weave a thread,
In laughter's wake, our worries shed.
Together strong, we brave the night,
In bonds unbroken, hearts take flight.

The river's bend, the ocean's waves,
In nature's song, our spirit saves.
Through winding paths, our stories blend,
In this embrace, we transcend.

With hands held tight, we face the skies,
In every storm, a love that flies.
Across the years, we'll dance, we'll sing,
In cascading joy, our souls take wing.

In fleeting moments, forever grown,
In every heartbeat, love has shone.
Together here, we'll find our way,
Cascading bonds that never fray.

Reflections in a Screen

In glassy depths, I find your face,
A mirrored soul in time and space.
With every flicker, memories gleam,
Reflections dance in a waking dream.

The words we type, a tender trace,
Of laughter shared, a warm embrace.
In filtered light, our secrets bloom,
As pixels weave through shadowed room.

Amidst the noise, our voices sound,
In every pause, true love is found.
Each scene unfolds, a vivid spark,
In glowing screens, we light the dark.

Through distant calls, we close the gap,
In every chat, a gentle map.
Your eyes, a window to my heart,
In digital realms, we'll never part.

So let the world outside grow dim,
In bright reflections, we'll begin.
A story told in frames of light,
Together always, through the night.

Bound by Distance

A stretch of sky between us wide,
The stars echo what we confide.
In whispers carried by the night,
Our dreams collide in silver light.

Though miles apart, our hearts align,
In seconds lost, you're still my sign.
Each sunset paints our paths anew,
In every hue, I'm close to you.

The ocean roars, the mountains grow,
Yet in the silence, love will flow.
A tether strong, though far we roam,
In the distance, we are home.

With hands extended in the air,
We bridge the gap, dissolve despair.
In laughter shared, in tears we've cried,
Through it all, love's never denied.

So let the miles fade into dreams,
For time will bend and break at seams.
In shadows cast and dawn's first light,
Forever bound, we rise in flight.

Unraveled Networks

Connections fray like threads of gold,
In tangled webs, our stories unfold.
With every click, a pulse ignites,
Across the void, we chase the lights.

Lost in a maze of endless streams,
Voices merged, we weave our dreams.
Pixel by pixel, we craft the scene,
In this vast world, where we've been.

Yet in the noise, we seek the song,
A harmony where we belong.
Through tangled lines, love finds its way,
A beacon bright, come what may.

In every share, a deeper glance,
In silent moments, we take a chance.
To bridge the gaps, to feel the spark,
In this vast net, we make our mark.

So let the currents pull us tight,
In tangled hearts, we feel the light.
For every distance that we cross,
In love's embrace, we gain, not loss.

Tangles of Time

In the folds of hours we entwine,
Moments lost, yet still divine.
A whisper held in heartbeat's note,
In tangled time, our dreams afloat.

Each second stretches, bends, then breaks,
In memories, the love awakes.
Days weave tapestries of the past,
Yet in the spiral, we hold fast.

Through shifting sands, we chase the day,
In every twilight, shadows play.
With every tick, we reel and sway,
In tangled time, we find our way.

A dance of years, a waltz unseen,
In echoes soft, our hearts convene.
Though clocks may chase, and seasons drift,
In gentle love, the world we gift.

So let us weave what cannot fray,
In this embrace, we choose to stay.
In tangled time, our story flows,
A timeless bond that ever grows.

Pixels that Yearn

In screens aglow, we reach and yearn,
With every scroll, our hearts unturned.
A silent spark in pixel's light,
We chase the shadows through the night.

The distance melts in glowing frames,
Creating bonds in whispered names.
In every post, a tale we share,
In vibrant joys, in silent prayer.

Yet still we seek beyond the glass,
Where real embraces come to pass.
In every moment, connection's pulse,
In boundless space, our dreams convulse.

In threads of time, we find our place,
Though worlds apart, we cross the space.
With every message sent and read,
Our hearts intertwine, where hope is bred.

So let the pixels speak our truth,
In every heart, the spark of youth.
For in the distance, love will learn,
In every glance, we come to yearn.

Where Souls Meet and Miss

In shadows cast where silence waits,
Two hearts will wane and hesitate.
A glance, a touch, the moments slip,
Across the void, they yearn to grip.

Yet echoes linger in the night,
When dreams entwine and hopes take flight.
A dance of fate, so close, so far,
In whispered wishes, they are scarred.

The tender threads of time unwind,
Two souls adrift, yet still aligned.
Through veils of doubt, they seek the spark,
In every silence, in the dark.

With every sigh, a heartbeat shared,
In distance felt, in moments bared.
Beyond the brush of fate's cruel hand,
They wander still, they understand.

For where they meet, the distance fades,
In shadowed glades, where love cascades.
Though missed at times, the bond remains,
In whispered names, through life's refrains.

The Layered Surface

Beneath the skin, a story lies,
With hidden paths and secret ties.
Those fleeting smiles, a painted grace,
Mask depths of thought in silent space.

Each layer thick with tales untold,
Of broken dreams and hearts of gold.
The surface glimmers, yet within,
A universe of where we've been.

In every glance, a world concealed,
A gentle touch, emotions healed.
Yet still we roam through life's façade,
Unraveling truths, at times so hard.

With every step, we peel away,
The shells we wear, the games we play.
Discovering what lies beneath,
In quiet moments, in belief.

So strip the layers, let love show,
In tender light, let feelings flow.
For in each heart, the scars define,
The laughter shared, the love divine.

Distorted Frequencies

In waves of sound, the truth distorts,
A melody of broken sorts.
The rhythm falters, time unravels,
With echoes lost on distant travels.

Through static air, our voices blend,
As frequency bends, we start to mend.
Connections formed in fractured ways,
Resonating in a tangled haze.

With every note, a tale we weave,
Yet in the noise, it's hard to grieve.
For harmony waits, just out of tune,
The moonlit skies, the glowing rune.

We search for clarity amidst the sound,
In whispers soft, where love is found.
Though signals clash and echoes fade,
The heart will map the paths we've laid.

So let us listen past the strife,
In dissonance, we find our life.
For in those frequencies, we'll find,
The songs of souls forever intertwined.

The Art of Unseen Bonds

In quiet glances, hearts align,
A dance of fate, both yours and mine.
With every word, unspoken thrives,
The silent ties that keep us alive.

Invisible threads, they softly weave,
A tapestry of dreams we conceive.
In laughter shared or tears we spill,
These bonds endure, they bend the will.

Through storms we pass, no need to speak,
For in the storm, our spirits peak.
With every challenge, hand in hand,
Unseen support, forever planned.

In moments still, where shadows blend,
A portrait formed that won't descend.
These ties unseen, yet ever strong,
A melody that we belong.

So cherish well the bonds we make,
In every choice, in every wake.
For in the art of love's embrace,
We find our home, our sacred space.

Fluid Lines of Communication

In whispers soft we share our tales,
Through channels deep as wind-filled sails.
Each heartbeat speaks, a silent tune,
Under the watchful gaze of the moon.

Thoughts cascade like streams so clear,
In every glance, our souls draw near.
Words like water, flowing free,
Carving paths eternally.

Bridges made of laughter bloom,
In every silence, there's room.
For understanding, a gentle grace,
In the space we choose to face.

Beneath the stars, stories collide,
With each breath, we must confide.
A dance of minds, a cosmic flight,
In the harmony of shared light.

Connection thrives in quiet threads,
Knots of trust where love spreads.
In fluid lines, we find our way,
A shared journey, come what may.

An Unraveled Yarn

Spools of color, twisted tight,
Each strand a story, pure delight.
With gentle hands, we pull and tease,
Winding together with relative ease.

In tangled knots, our past remains,
Frayed edges holding joy and pains.
Every loop, a memory spun,
In threads of laughter, we are one.

A tapestry of moments bright,
Woven patterns in morning light.
Unraveled tales, yet still we weave,
In every breath, we find reprieve.

Old fibers bridge the gaps of time,
In rhythmic beats, a subtle rhyme.
With colors bold, we paint our days,
In vibrant strokes, our hearts ablaze.

Though yarns may fray, we hold them near,
In every stitch, a whispered cheer.
Creating warmth, we break apart,
For in the chaos lies true art.

The Silence of Traffic

Amidst the rush, a stillness lies,
In honking horns and bustling skies.
The world races, yet here I stand,
Absorbing peace, a quiet land.

Engines growl, tires hum their tune,
Yet in the chaos, I find my rune.
A moment holds, suspended grace,
In fleeting time, this sacred space.

In every pause, a breath of air,
The pulse of life, a vibrant flare.
As lights flicker like stars above,
I find connection, I find love.

Echoes of life, a symphony,
Underneath the urban canopy.
In silence thick, the stories weave,
Through every heartbeat, we believe.

Traffic shifts, a river of fate,
In waiting rooms, we contemplate.
In every honk, a chance to feel,
In borrowed time, the world is real.

The Dissonance of Proximity

In crowded rooms, the echoes swell,
A cacophony where whispers dwell.
Bodies close yet miles apart,
In the clamor, a fractured heart.

Faces brush, but eyes don't meet,
In fleeting glances, we retreat.
The noise surrounds, a heavy cloud,
Yet inside, we long to be loud.

Strangers dance in tangled air,
Lost connections everywhere.
A symphony of disarray,
In harmony, we drift away.

Each conversation, half-expressed,
In proximity, we feel the stress.
A longing spark, yet silence reigns,
In the closeness, the distance pains.

With every step, we crave the bond,
Yet in the midst, we often abscond.
For dissonance is what we find,
In crowded spaces, hearts unwind.

The Space Between Us

In shadows cast by our own fears,
We drift apart through silent years.
The stars will flicker, lost in time,
Yet hope ignites, a whispered rhyme.

A breath, a glance, we dare not share,
Two souls adrift in a tender air.
Each heartbeat echoes, a deafening song,
Yet we hold tight, as if we belong.

The moonlight bathes our separate paths,
In dreams we linger, without the masks.
What bridges built in quiet grace,
Can span the void, this empty space?

Together yet apart we stand,
With outstretched arms, we form a band.
Through every distance, a bond we weave,
In the space between, we still believe.

Let time converge, let worries cease,
In the harmony of our shared peace.
For in every longing, there lies a trust,
A world awaits, beyond the rust.

Boundaries of Belonging

In circles drawn by hearts' design,
We seek the place where we align.
Yet borders mark this fragile land,
Where dreams collide, hand in hand.

What holds us close can keep us lost,
In boundaries built, we bear the cost.
The yearning whispers, soft and clear,
To break the walls and draw us near.

Yet every line we dare to cross,
Is marked by love, a gain, a loss.
In open fields where spirits soar,
We challenge space forevermore.

Through veils of doubt, we find a way,
To reshape the night into day.
In every heart, a chance to grow,
Together strong, we overflow.

In this realm of give and take,
We learn the art of every ache.
Each boundary fades, as love expands,
In sacred trust, where life commands.

Invisible Lattices

Beneath the surface, threads entwined,
Invisible bonds of heart and mind.
Weaving secrets, a tapestry bright,
In every laugh, in every fright.

The lattice hums with silent grace,
A web of voices left to trace.
Through woven paths, we find our way,
In every night, and in each day.

What cannot be seen holds the weight,
Of promises forged by fate.
With gentle hands, we shape and steer,
In every binding, our souls draw near.

These threads may strain, yet never break,
A dance of longing, for connection's sake.
In every heart, a structure grows,
Invisible lattices, love bestows.

So let us trust the ties we make,
In every moment, the chance to wake.
For in this net, we are not alone,
Together we rise, to claim our own.

Harmonies of Disconnection

In melodies where silence reigns,
We find the notes of our refrains.
Though distance stretches, chords can blend,
In harmonies, our souls ascend.

Each word left unspoken can sing,
In a symphony that time will bring.
For every parting, a tune will swell,
In the quiet, where echoes dwell.

We dance in shadows, we learn to sway,
Through disconnection, we find our way.
Each step apart, a rhythm seeks,
In the beats of hearts, the language speaks.

A distant strum, a gentle pull,
In every silence, harmony's full.
Though miles divide, the music flows,
Uniting worlds, as passion grows.

So let us cherish what time creates,
The laughter shared, the lonely fates.
In every chord, a spark ignites,
In harmonies of disconnection, we find our lights.

Signals Lost in Translation

Words drift like leaves in the breeze,
Echoes of meaning fade with ease.
In the silence, whispers collide,
Messages lost, nowhere to hide.

Eyes search for truth in a crowded room,
But gestures falter, and doubts loom.
Bridges built from fragile intent,
Crumbled by phrases misrepresent.

Fingers type with hearts that betray,
Nuances tangled in wires' fray.
In the void, connections strain,
Familiar faces, yet none remain.

Hope flickers like a distant star,
Guiding us close, though we're far.
In a world where words break apart,
Feelings linger in every heart.

Yet still we reach, through the flawed space,
Finding echoes of love's embrace.
Though signals fail and meanings blur,
In the silence, our souls stir.

The Distance Between Us

Miles stretch like shadows in the night,
Every heartbeat a whispered fight.
Photographs gather dust on the shelf,
Memories fade as we lose ourselves.

Voices crackle through the phone,
In the silence, we both feel alone.
Eyes that once sparkled seem dim,
The distance grows, the light grows slim.

Starlit skies know our shared dreams,
Yet time unravels at the seams.
Hopes exchanged beneath the moon,
Yet longing's song starts to croon.

Every step feels heavy, restrained,
Trying to bridge the love that remained.
But oceans lie between every touch,
The taste of longing, it's all too much.

Still, I chase the memory of your smile,
Counting seconds, mile by mile.
In this vast world, you're still my guide,
Through the distance, love won't subside.

Silent Links

In the quiet spaces, you are here,
Echoes of laughter, whispers near.
The air vibrates with unspoken ties,
Every glance a truth that never lies.

Hands brush lightly, a fleeting touch,
In silence, we connect so much.
With a breath, a shared sigh,
Words unneeded, just you and I.

Moments linger like the fading light,
In the hush, our souls unite.
Laughter dances in the evening air,
In stillness, we find a bond so rare.

Every heartbeat becomes a song,
In this quiet, where we belong.
Invisible threads pull tighter still,
In silence, your presence fills.

We weave our dreams with unsaid fears,
In the silence, love appears.
Together in this tranquil space,
Two souls bound with gentle grace.

The Pulse of Pixels

Fingers hover over screens so bright,
In a world of pixels, lost from sight.
Each notification, a heartbeat's call,
Yet shadows linger beneath it all.

Smiles ignited through digital streams,
But behind the glass, reality seems.
Typing fast, thoughts rush by,
Yet real connections begin to die.

Scrolling through memories, lost in feeds,
In every pixel, a story bleeds.
Hearts connect, yet drift away,
In the network's web, we lose our way.

But somewhere deep, a pulse remains,
In the data flow, love sustains.
Through the noise, we still persevere,
Finding warmth in a virtual sphere.

So here's to the links that spark our fire,
In the coded world, we still aspire.
To bridge the gaps with each soft click,
In the pulse of pixels, our hearts tick.

Bound by Ones and Zeros

In a world of code we dwell,
Each bit a tale, a silent spell.
Connections spark with every click,
In binary code, we find our flick.

Across the waves, our voices fly,
Invisible threads, we laugh and sigh.
Yet, still alone, we hold our screens,
The silent space where no one leans.

Data flows like rivers wide,
In endless bytes, we must confide.
Moments shared through glowing light,
Yet shadows haunt the endless night.

Pixels dance in vibrant hues,
Telling stories, tangled views.
We bind ourselves in lines we trace,
Seeking solace in this space.

But deep within the flickering glow,
A longing stirs, a need to know.
Beyond the zeros, beyond the ones,
A heart waits still while fast life runs.

Tangled Roots and Wi-Fi

Beneath the ground, the roots entwine,
Whispering secrets, old as time.
In tangled webs, we search for heights,
Connected here, beneath the sights.

Wi-Fi signals, waves in air,
Bridges built, we venture there.
Yet still we cling to ancient ground,
As digital echoes swirl around.

The soil holds memories so dear,
Each drop of rain, each whispered cheer.
In every network, stories bloom,
Roots and branches, a shared room.

Yet in this web, we may forget,
The laughter shared, the tears unmet.
Screens replace the warmth of touch,
In wireless worlds, we crave so much.

So let us pause, look deep within,
Find solace free from where we've been.
For tangled roots will guide us back,
To paths where love will never lack.

The Pulse of Interconnection

Through wires and waves, our hearts align,
A pulse that beats, a lifeline sign.
In every click, a spark ignites,
In silent nights, our spirit writes.

The hum of servers, a rhythmic sound,
In every heartbeat, we're tightly bound.
From distant lands, we share a gaze,
In every click, we forge our ways.

Yet amid the surge, we drift away,
Lost in the ether, we often sway.
Connections thrive but often fray,
In this vast web, where hearts can stray.

We seek each other in this vast sea,
Yet loneliness lurks deceptively.
In virtual realms, we find our peace,
But crave the warmth that won't decease.

So let us bridge the digital space,
With every heartbeat, find our place.
And let our stories intertwine,
In this great pulse, our hearts align.

TLS: Trust, Loneliness, and Solitude

In tunnels guarded, secrets flow,
A layer trusted, we come to know.
Yet still, beneath the lines we trace,
Lies loneliness in digital space.

Fractured whispers, connection speaks,
Yet every heartbeat, silence seeks.
In solitude, we often find,
A mirror reflecting a distant mind.

Through encrypted paths, we share our dreams,
But shadows linger in silent streams.
Trust forged in data, yet fragile still,
In every message, a longing will.

Can we untangle the webs we weave?
Find warmth in hearts, allow to grieve?
For solitude wears a heavy cloak,
In every laugh, a hidden joke.

So let us reach beyond the screen,
In search of moments of what has been.
For trust can blossom in the light,
When hearts connect, we will ignite.

Faded Frequencies

Whispers in the air, so thin,
Lost echoes where dreams begin.
Signals flicker, dimmed and frail,
In silence deep, we set our sail.

Static noise of yesterday,
Hiding truths we can't relay.
Waves that crash on distant shores,
Fade away, and close the doors.

Melodies of a life once bright,
Now are shadows, lost in flight.
In the void, we seek a sign,
Faded frequencies entwine.

In the mist, we walk alone,
Searching for a softer tone.
Time will weave its silver thread,
In memories of things unsaid.

As we drift on life's ocean wide,
Faded frequencies abide.
Hearts will try to find their tune,
Beneath a distant, waning moon.

Mindscapes of Isolation

In corridors of thought, we roam,
Designing rooms that feel like home.
Each shadow holds a whispered fear,
In solitude, the mind draws near.

Walls of silence, tall and stark,
Reflecting echoes, bright and dark.
Fleeting glimpses of what could be,
Fragments lost in reverie.

A canvas painted in shades of grey,
Dreams and memories drift away.
In solitude, we learn to fight,
To find our voices in the night.

Thoughts collide like waves at sea,
Building castles made of glee.
In this mindscape, shadows play,
Light and dark, they weave and sway.

With every step, the heart will mend,
In isolation, we transcend.
Building bridges to the sun,
Mindscapes bloom, we're not undone.

Whirlwinds of Thought

Spinning fast like autumn leaves,
In the chaos, the heart believes.
Thoughts like storms, they twist and twine,
In the whirlwind, I seek a sign.

Restless skies, a tempest wild,
Within the storm, the mind's a child.
Questions whirl in blinding speed,
In the dance, we plant a seed.

Racing shadows, fleeting light,
Peace and turmoil, day and night.
Every breath, a chance to soar,
In this whirlwind, we explore.

Casting nets in turbulent streams,
Catching shards of broken dreams.
Among the storms, we find our place,
In the whirlwinds, we embrace.

Thoughts will settle, calm will reign,
In silence, we break the chain.
Rising stronger through the fight,
Whirlwinds carve our paths to light.

Intersections of Solitude

Paths converge in quiet places,
Whispers trace forgotten faces.
At the crossroads, hearts reside,
In solitude, we must confide.

Each road taken, steps unplanned,
In loneliness, we try to stand.
Voices echo through the dark,
Finding solace in a spark.

Moments linger like fading stars,
Carving maps of silent scars.
Through the haze, we witness grace,
At the intersections we embrace.

Choices made with cautious breath,
Life and longing dance with death.
In stillness, shadows intertwine,
Through solitude, we learn to shine.

Yet every crossing holds a key,
Unlocking what's inside of me.
In solitude's embrace, we find,
Intersections of the mind.

Conversations in the Void

Whispers echo in the dark,
Silent shadows drift apart.
Thoughts collide without a sound,
In this space where dreams are found.

Stars connect in cosmic dance,
Infinite realms of fleeting chance.
Minds entwined across the air,
Lost in realms beyond compare.

Voices linger, softly fade,
In the silence, truths are laid.
Breathe the light of vacant skies,
In the void, no goodbye lies.

Fragments pulse like distant light,
Guiding hearts through endless night.
The unseen ties that weave us whole,
Converse in whispers of the soul.

What we share, a fleeting touch,
In this void, we find so much.
Conversations drift and sway,
In the dark, we find our way.

Stitches of the Digital Quilt

Pixels scatter, weave and blend,
Stories told, no clear end.
Patterns form in vivid hues,
Each thread a tale, a path we choose.

In the web of screens we find,
Connections forged, both heart and mind.
Stitches of laughter, tears, and fears,
A tapestry of all our years.

Code like language, soft and bright,
Crafting worlds in day and night.
Every heartbeat, every glance,
Seams of longing in this dance.

Quilted memories, soft embrace,
Holding worlds in cyber space.
Weaving dreams with every click,
Threads of peace, and moments thick.

Together we exist, apart,
Each connection, a beating heart.
In this digital expanse, we shall,
Sew together, rise and fall.

Static Currents

Frequencies bounce like restless waves,
Static hums where silence braves.
Interference in the air we share,
Voices caught in electric flair.

Wires hum with untold tales,
Echoes swirl, like shipset sails.
Between the lines, a pulse ignites,
A hidden world in dark delights.

Neon lights and shadows play,
In this current, minds give sway.
Digital whispers weave and twist,
In the static, we persist.

Rhythms surge in tangled paths,
Threads of thought that lightning casts.
In the noise, we find a song,
A heartbeat prompting us along.

Ride the waves of time and space,
In electric dreams, we'll trace.
Static currents binding tight,
In this flow, we spark the light.

Unseen Handshakes

In the quiet corners, hearts convene,
Unseen handshakes, soft and keen.
Connections bloom without a word,
Silent agreements, rarely heard.

Glimpses shared in fleeting glances,
Moments frozen, chance advances.
A nod exchanged, a pulse ignites,
In the shadowed dance of lights.

Trust flows like a river wide,
Carving paths where fears abide.
We navigate this subtle space,
With gentle gestures, we embrace.

In silence loud, we find our way,
In the unseen, we learn to stay.
Hand in hand, though out of sight,
We create our world in light.

Every heartbeat, every sign,
Strength in bonds that intertwine.
Unseen handshakes, soft as air,
In the quiet, strength we share.

Milton Keynes UK
Ingram Content Group UK Ltd.
UKHW022004131124
451149UK00013B/999